A PERFECT LITTLE GIFT
POETRY AND PROSE

BY **TONY ROBINSON OBE**

CREATED AND INTRODUCED
BY **TARYN LEE JOHNSTON**

A PERFECT LITTLE GIFT

POETRY & PROSE

BY TONY ROBINSON OBE

CREATED & INTRODUCED BY
TARYN LEE JOHNSTON

Featuring:
A small selection of popular poems written between 1969 and 2021

&

A concise explanation of the Soculitherz' Incredible-Choco-Wine Diet

Copyright © Tony Robinson OBE, 2019
Published: October 2019 by Chronos Publishing
Second Edition Published December 2021

ISBN: 978 – 0-9955943 – 0-2 Paperback Edition
ISBN: 978 – 0-9955943 – 1-9 e-book Edition

All rights reserved.

The right of Tony Robinson OBE to be identified as author of this Work has been asserted by him in accordance with sections 77 and 78 of the Copyright, Designs and Patents Act 1988.

No part of this publication may be reproduced, stored in retrieval system, copied in any form or by any means, electronic, mechanical, photocopying, recording or otherwise transmitted without written permission from the publisher. You must not circulate this book in any format.

Cover design by Danjis Designs

INTRODUCTION BY TARYN LEE JOHNSTON

I have the pleasure of co-editing this book and selecting from Tony's work, this includes poems dating back to his very early days of writing, almost fifty years ago, to his latest verse, a few tweets and a song penned during the pandemic. I've also included extracts from his published, satire novels and of course the infamous Soculitherz, *Incredible Choco-Wine diet.*

When studying for his English and American Literature degree, nearly fifty years ago, Tony handed a lecturer a folder containing over a hundred poems and a 3 Act Play. He asked the lecturer to tell him what she thought of his writing. A few weeks later he had a response. His writing was *"Of no literary merit"*.

Being a publisher, I know how deeply reviews can discourage a writer and so, I am delighted that Tony didn't allow that opinion to curtail his love of prose.

I have come to know Tony and his writing very well over the last few years, as we co-authored **'The Happipreneur'**—the new *Small Is Beautiful*—a guide for enterprising people everywhere. During this time, I have become aware of his delightful sense of humour and turn of phrase.

This book was initially designed for friends and family and it is a rare and precious insight into a quirky yet beautiful mind!

His first published poem was 'Circles' and there are two others from fifty years ago: 'Seventeen' and 'Clowns'.

As a lover of poetry and literature, it's wonderful to see both brought together here in his work, combined with the, at times innocent way he views the world and those within his closest circle.

The prose here is both a public service and an indulgence for me and fans of the entirely mythical fashionista, investigative reporter and creator of the Incredible Choco-Wine Diet—Ms Leonora Soculitherz.

I challenge anyone to try the Choco-Wine Diet for themselves, after all what's not to love about chocolate and wine...?

Tony is currently on a 70 'Who Wants To Be A Happipreneur?' Shows' virtual and live events tour for his 70th year.

He is raising funds from the show for #Exclude-dUK Boost Grants. In tandem with the Shows, he is completing 70x7 mile runs, including a half marathon and a marathon.

These runs are to raise funds for Macmillan Cancer Support.

Please contact Tony directly if you'd like to donate.

CONTENTS

POETRY
(1969 – 2021)

GETTING THERE

How? How? How? How?
Well, well, well, well
Boom, boom, boom, boom
Gonna shoot you right down
Right off your feet
Doctor
Take away all you got

Chop, chop, chop, chop
Bang, bang, bang, bang
Buy your ticket to ride the two seas-
Sahara and Aegean—babies come free
Teacher
To Lesvos, Lampedusa, Malta and Sicily

Flip-flop, flip-flop
Boom, boom, boom, boom
There's camping too
Exit with a crowd floating light
At the dead of night
Business owner
Wait and pray—they'll find you

Sick, Sick, Sick, Sick
Bang, bang, bang, bang
Never gonna let you down, up or in
Bombed, shot, hacked, diseased
Tortured and drowned
Artist
Another jungle fevered head in the wall

Dante, Dante, Dante, Dante
Boom, boom, boom, boom
How? How? How? How?

TIME IS MY TRAIN

On my seat is a number
My window gobbles
Sights seen then forgotten
Whoosh
My number is passed on
To the next passenger
On the only trip
People get ready

Flying is faster
On light summer nights
Driving is scary
On dark winter nights
Fear falling and bends
On my table I play
Snakes and ladders
And pick-up sticks
Chewing and dropping
Jigsaw pieces

On the way out
I shout LOUD
I will not
B QUIET
Turn it off
Go away
Go to the next carriage
Disembark
Whoosh

WOW!

Wow! He does look old now
Spotlight on silver hair
Pink cheeks puffed below
Reading glasses.

Wow! He does look old now
Start gets a laugh
Collar looks tight on
Talking head

Wow! He does look old now
One hand fiddles whilst
The other grips tight
Squeezing time

Wow! He does look old now
Slivers of sweat from
Forehead to nose drops
Wetting lips

Wow! He does look old now
Lost in his notes
Rushing to finish
Clapped—respectfully

Wow! He does look old now
Back to his seat
Safe in his job
Earning living

THIRD

One year
As a schoolboy
Twice I came
Third in the shot put
Third sucks
Third hurts
Third is nowt to write home about
4
Sportspeople, musicians, politicians, applicants
Customers, competitors, trades
people, actors, barristers
&
Lovers

SEAPLAY

Pierced and wired for sound scream
up, down, round and round

Laughing policemen scare as
sucking slots are stuffed senseless

Rednecks gaze and gobble on
scarred seats, in memoriam

Yellow stained thumbs scorch in
smoking cans or sodden sand

Hip hats, wobbly vests and saggy
shorts flip flop by

Shades in deckchairs lined in black
and white of gore and guilt

Hey you over there! Come closer

Zoltar can tell your fortune
For a small fee

Enjoy yourself, it's later than you think

Lazy, snuggled bodies stretch and sigh

Tupperware treats on car seats

Ice cream noses and candy floss hair

Sticky hands touch and squeeze

Yachts crewed by dandy dudes

City slickers sup and surf

Bright, light, blue, pink and orange

Friendly waves kiss sandy toes

Reflections giggle back

See them play

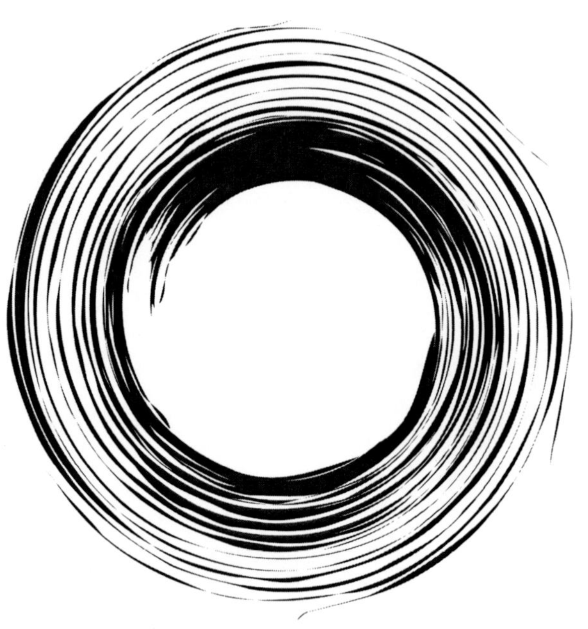

CIRCLES

Never ending circles
Round, round and round
Raindrop plops
Brick thwacks
Volcano erupts
Sounds
Whirling
Never ending circles
Revolving
Evolving
In a puddle, pond, lake and sea
Round and round and
People born and murdered
Without a sound
Circles of lies and theft
Dropped
Stopped
Hold hard breath
Calm
Frenzy
Break free
Which way?
Can you see?
Never ending circles
Round, round and round

ALL RATHER COLOURFUL

Lights were red
Mind said go
Legs led
Road slowed

I streamed my thoughts
They gave no clue
Flying high
Tied up too

Accelerating quickly
Without moving an inch
Feeling so silly
At a pinch

The white line grew
Into a wall
I stared aghast
I'm not that tall

Quickly I flew
The wall smiled
It would do
I'm toast
My white coffin was carried
By ladies in green
My bride never married
Didn't seem bothered

Mourners in yellow
Were laughing aloud
A few could not bellow
Stuffing food

Some prayed for forgiveness
A few applauded my sins
The speeches were rubbish
Hadn't learned a thing

The grass was green
The earth was brown
The box went down
Nowt more to be seen

ME UNCLE RON

Me Uncle Ron raced me Uncle Trev
From pillow to lamppost to field
To feed horses, then raced back
Before school

Me Uncle Ron and Uncle Trev
Saw hills of rubble
Next to their street
In Hull. Friends dead.

Me Uncle Ron measured the same
As Randolph Turpin and jabbed
And feinted and hooked and ducked
Day in and day out.

Me Uncle Ron was sickly forever
Pound a round was good money then
Sick of boxing, sick of being hit
By a drunken Dad.

Me Uncle Ron fled to the medical corps
Jab, jab, faint, faint
Blood on canvas and death
Bucket loads
Me Uncle Ron met me at my house
He lived there with his sister, me Mum
Me Dad couldn't breathe—sawdust and cigs
Dad kicked him out

Me Uncle Ron lived in the biggest block
Of flats that you've ever seen
He killed a man once with his forklift truck
On the docks he was known for never drinking,
Never smoking and never having mates.
He was my hero.

Me Uncle Ron had skin like tissue paper
Every knock meant he bled and bled
One day he bled enough to fill his bath
He drank whisky that day.
He told me he would
In the crem there was me and Uncle Trev and
Uncle Ron in a box—no service or nothing.

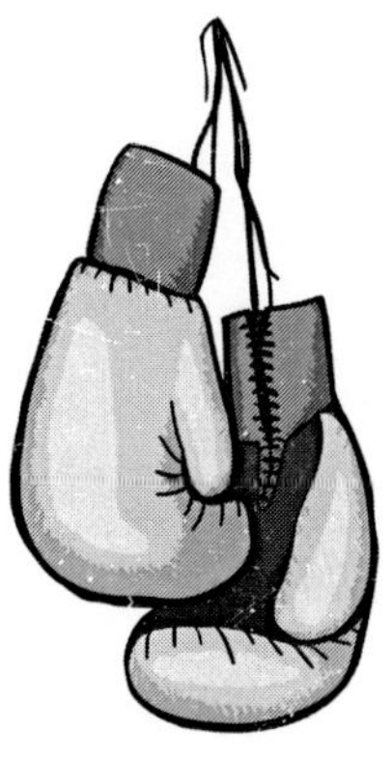

NO, YOU DON'T KNOW

I have a best friend
The kindest person
I know
Works very hard
I know
Never needed to work
I know more
Because she teaches me
More than
I knew before
Every time we meet
I listen better now
I know
It hurts deep
When people think they know you
By your speech

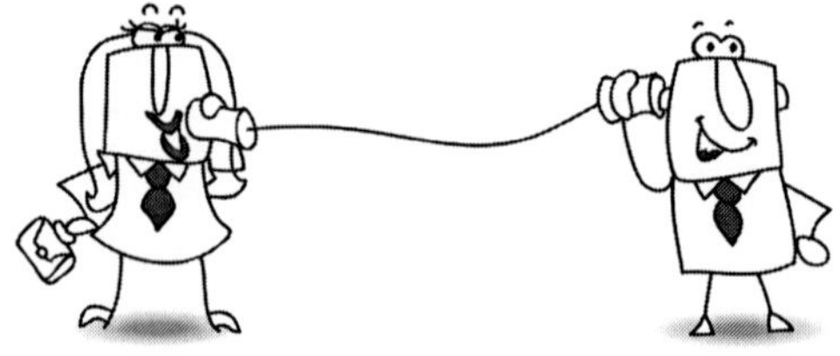

CLOWNS

Send in the
Scary clowns and narky jesters
Suit and boot the leery fools
Bring on the
Bored actors and dead comedians
Conning, politicking and robbing
Show me
No act
No laughs
No heart
No make-up cracked.
No better times
No more
No reason
A fool still
A false stage
A trap door
A sickly circus
Of smiles
To curse
To damn
To praise
For recompense
Should fools live alone?
Stop playing?
Stop?
There's no business
Like your own business

HOW MANY MORE TIMES?

I'm right, aren't I?
Yet again
I knew this would happen
You do this every time
Open your eyes
For once—engage brain
Wind me up
Why not?
You know how to get me going
God
Do I deserve this?
Well I'm not going to stand for it
Much longer
You can think yourself lucky
This is it

FLAILING

Near the top of Mount Etna
You glimpse
How dwellings are stolen
How waves are irresistible
We can only flail and stir

Hubble bubble boiling broth
Of oil
Pouring trouble on everything
Everywhere
We can only flail and despair

The vines filibuster into the gaps
Fertile
Beneath the roars and screams
Neither cleansed nor washed away
We can only flail and tear our hair

09:30
MY PHOTOS
DATA
SEARCH

IPHONE

iPhone is intuitive technology
I power off

ISaw there's a vibrator that the partner
remote controls
I daren't

IGaming is addictive for euphoria seekers
I prefer stacking chips on 17

ISounds through earphones silence nature
I don't do naturism

IDinners seem to be mostly vegan
I wouldn't kill for a tofu

IExplore landscapes and mindscapes daily
I never know where

IContact often delights but there are no
eyes in Facebook

ICan laugh, love and scream silently
I die

There's an app for that

TWINS

My year at Beverley Grammar School
Had twins
Two of them—boys
Big friends of my doubles partner
He married their sister
We won tennis matches by lobbing
High into the sun
We're all 67-ish
When I was 16
Fell in love with a twin—girls
Never knew which one
At Butlins—girls
One week is not enough
They all say that—boys
My fave twins work at Kings Cross
Articulate and attractive
Women
Holograms
Looking after twin elevators
Always there
Preventing accidents
I love the twin on the left
The twin on the right is moody
I keep going left
Right makes my day
Up and down—laughing inside
Always a big smile
Hers and mine

Usually a wave
Sometimes she beckons
Of course, I go
Sometimes I hide behind someone
Or a sign
Just to see if I'm spotted
I am
She looks out for me
Nods in recognition
I nod back
Twinkles her eyes
I can't do that
And smiles
Ooh 'eck—twins eh?

YOU'RE PULLING MY PLONKER

If you'd been there
You would have loved it
They talked a bit
About your
Writing, music,
woodwork, jewellery
and photos
You knew what they'd say
I know your poems they daren't read out
X-rated eulogies
aren't cool yet
Sanitised memories instead
Artefacts of your brilliant mind.
magical hands,
artistic eyes.
Me—your curator
Them—a shower
People you
never talked about,
even a bit.
Panel beater to videographer
Maintenance and facilities manager
and pick pack line fixer
Never applied but
always determined
to
get it right, Fred
Each project
nailed

Like solving genius
crossword puzzles
They seemed in a rush
I longed for
more minutes,
with a pint,
of your
irreverence
Epic-every time
What would I say?
What would you say?
Craggy and black?
Laconic and blue?
Always right
Fred said
what he knew
was true
What he foresaw
Which I didn't see
Common sense
So uncommon
Left to do
without your truth
How dare they
bring their clichés
You should have been there
Who's pulling what?

SEVENTEEN

In nine hundred and fifty-three
My courtly lady beckoned me
To Castle Comfort over a black stream
I was sure the moat smiled, and a door screamed

She led me into a fine banqueting room
Strange to see everything painted blue
it was early morning, but it seemed like night
No food, no windows, no candles, no light

I must have seemed puzzled for she answered my
gaze
'Don't worry my lord, life is much better without
days'
I asked if this meant she knew of no time
'Yes, this way we live and love', she replied

I said, 'But how can one live without any light?'
'I'll show you my Lord, you pretend that it's night.
Ask me your questions whilst were in bed'
She made love so well I slept instead

I awoke much later, the light was too bright for
my eyes
I cried out in wonder, but my lady slept on by my
side
She woke, then she kissed me for days
Then said 'Now you see how dark and time fly
away'

I soon understood this Castle of moods
Unhappy thoughts brought rain, darkness and
turned everything blue
Joy brought sunshine, laughter and gaily coloured
things
It really was too wonderful a world to stop and
think

But one day in the Garden of Trust
I asked my lady why all this should happen to us
She said, 'By courtly tradition we did our pen-
ance.
We fought dragons of heartbreak and were
tortured by silence.

We beat lions of deceit and giants of sorrow
Scorned time that had passed, loving now not
tomorrow.
Until at last we understood life well enough.
Our reward is an endless life in this Castle of love'

'Yet, then there's one thing I cannot quite see -
why did you arrive here before me?'
She answered, 'See my apple tree over there.
Once you dare not taste sweetness but fed on
despair.

Whilst it took you years to trust
It took me as long to learn how to love
You came here to me in nine hundred and

fifty-three
The year is now nine hundred and seventy

For 17 years we've lived here my dear
This last one was the happiest year
This castle is getting much stronger
The birds sing much longer'

She brought my hand to her golden hair
Kissed me warm and sweetly and whispered a
prayer
'Was that prayer about me?'
'Yes indeed, I hope you love me, not my fantasy'

ONE SAINT JUDE

Not had much luck
Spotting Saints
Just the three
One was my philosophy lecturer
Became Chief Rabbi
Then a Lord
Barred from sainthood, obviously

Two was one of my Aunties—Dolly and Annie
Lived in a prefab in Hull
Dolly looked after Annie
Auntie Dolly's body was bent
She was so old—about my age now
And I was seven
So, I didn't record her miracles
Like bowling mystery off spin
For hours
To knock my forward defensive
Into shape

Which just leaves
Three, the only one that counts
Saint Jude of Willerby High Street
Where Saints are not plentiful
So, it was a right good spot
By me of this 16-year-old Saint

Willerby High Street Saints
Don't use their halos

They use mugs of coffee
As she hands you a mug
She tells you 'what's what'
Sorts you out
Dry cleans you
Stands up for you
Suffers ridicule
Stifles bullies
Shows you the way
To help all the people
Everyone else
Avoids
One Saint Jude
Of
Many safe havens

SO LONG GOLDEN VOICE
(2021)

So long golden voice
They wanted it darker
Crashing, warming, infecting, bombing
Oranges die down by the plastic river
Rich get richer, poor get punished
Everybody knows
Slogans jam the airwaves
Harmony behind our backs
Heartfelt fedoras on parallel tracks
Rocking seventies on tour
Third act last gasps
Time to floor the tower of wrong
There are no secrets—do ron, ron, ron
Song survived sin and longing
Hallelujah
Doing what you love
That's how the light gets in

TWENTY FEET ASUNDER
(2021)

Not a D'Urberville just a laughing Labrador
Unhurried. never sad, a champion snacker
Her vet was overweight too—who knew?
Leisure is for life and walks are for food
Waiting was her superpower
Expectant eyes, a smelting smile
Tail wags till they donate her booty
All will surrender, even the mean and snooty
Row by row of deck chairs relent
There's ice cream in the cornet ends
Outside the pub crunching crisps
Washed down with Shandy
Snuggled together waiting for Daddy

Not Mr Bojangles' just jumped so high
Dancer, catcher, speedster, flier
Blink and she was gone
Clap and she was back
Nonplussed. enthused, a labra-whippet
Overthinking? She never did it
Shunned as undogly
Happiness is family
Named after a Hull Fair fish
Hoover of floors, cleaner of dishes
Never an oldie, always a kid
With crazy dreams at warp speed
Didn't up and die when skin and bones

Our lie, stroked, jabbed, a sigh
Gone in seconds, humane, her joy remains

Not a jungle cat just not to be messed with
Glad to be on his side but better not say so
Team sports and huddles he never did
Mr Big but never a Six-Dinner Sid—like me
The move to the seaside was not his plan
Took a sabbatical and then some
Brought back but not bothered
Didn't look sickly—harbour food?
Swapped the Romany life for Security
As in serious guarding from intruders,
Cats and dogs, our friends or foes,
and neighbours
Working out, flexing, slowly stalking,
staring coldly
An occasional mauling screamed out a warning
To those that dared test the best in his profession.
I think he liked us

Not the Terminator just a big,
loud body with six-inch legs
Other dogs, cats and plumbers think he is
Black? Dog? Irish? Immigrant? Yes!
Must have had my dealer
Made by a Westie Mum and Bouvier Dad
Superior, smart, besuited, revered,
wise and condescending
Champion of diversity but speaks little French
for a Belgian

Tending cows is his profession
Lack of cows in Scarbados township
Means he herds us instead
His eighties are painful,
each day is a flickering fire
Monsieur Le Shag will not retire.

Not a head for heights just for admiring
Dyspraxia is cruel to the beautiful
Yawn, sleepy stretch and bed fall
Stairs are flying fun and bumpy rides
A feline princess with a sore crown
Feet are for cleaning not for landing
The way you got up can never be found
Curious eyes see no safe route to ground
Black dog makes her anxious
Great outdoors makes her fractious
Her grace is best when motionless
Her vocation is allure, so not ambitious
Playtime, belly rubs, warmth, sleep, affection,
Sustenance and home is a quietly,
comfy condition

***TOO OLD
(TWEET APRIL 2020)***

Time's up

You've had your lot

Had your go

Think of others

Save Lives

Don't be selfish

Take it on the chin

Stay alert

Out of sight

Whack-a-mole

Sign this

Why?

State pension?

Tick

Not self-sufficient?

Tick

Underlying Condition?

Tick

Old?

Tick

DNR?

Tick

...Tock

NO BUSINESS
(TWEET JUNE 2020)

There's NO business
Like your own business
Like no business I know
Everything about it was so appealing

BUT no business owner
Survives a Govt beating
3 million are
@ExcludedUK
Sobbing over bills to pay
Nowt from months of pleading

BLOW after blow
Sickened by BJ's
No show

MENTALISM
(TWEET—JULY 2021)

Not a wand
An injection
By wizards
Shuffling decks
Hopeless

Not a circus
A sketch
By Boz
Hard Times
Enrichment

Not a bus
A lie
About millions
Gangbusters
Duped

Not a book
Animal welfare
Open gates
Whack-a-mole
Spread

Not a puppet
A suit
Spun gold
"Sadly"

SONG FOR BJ—DON'T THINK TWICE IT'S OUR LIVES (JUNE 2020)

Well, it ain't no use to hide and lie, BJ
We know Dom's game by now
And it ain't no use to hide and lie, BJ
Too many dead, anyhow
When your masters call for their pot of gold
Don't say you spent it killing the old
You're the reason our blood runs cold
Don't think twice, it's all life

And it ain't no use herding the poor, BJ
They don't listen anymore
And it ain't no use purging the sick, BJ
Your doctors gonna lock the door
When they tug your strings to shine their shoes
You best be giving 'em women and booze
You killed our livelihoods and we got
nothing to lose
Don't think twice, it's our life

And it ain't no use sending 'em home, BJ
A home they never knew
And it ain't no use calling them names, BJ
Just cos they don't look like you
So when they come a-knocking to hand over
the keys
You'd better learn to kneel, say sorry and please

We just know that we can't breathe
Don't think twice it's our lives

Hey, you're just so King Kong, BJ
That smirk you wear so well
Yeah, you're the biggest swinging dick, BJ
Your stand up trumps our yells
Now we ain't saying that you were the boss
But you tell all the lies so humanity lost
You just Christmas partied without giving a toss
Don't think twice, it's our lives

A LONELY LIFE
TARYN LEE JOHNSTON 2021

It's 10pm and you should have gone to bed
In fact, a while ago
But there's so much to do in your head
So that won't happen
Your days are filled with fear and dread
But that's not stopping you
You'll quiet the demons that plague you instead
By smothering them
In gin, or wine, until the muse is fed
With creation

It's lonely and exhausting being self employed
But so very powerful
Days merge into weeks into months into voids
Tick tock tick tock
You ask why? Am I gaining or unemployed?
Neither and sometimes both
A bright moment of success cuts through the
noise
A moment to smile but you're too busy
Beating yourself up for a mistake you didn't avoid
One that only you saw

But it's a wonderful thing to be a Happipreneur
If you know what that is
A freedom of spirit, a life connoisseur
A problem solver
Ideas, challenges, bright sparks as it were
Standing, still standing
Yes, it's lonely at times but I know what I prefer
And yes, maybe I'll go to bed, soon
But there's a man in a red hat to you I'll refer
He knows the truth and is prepared to share.

PROSE

THE ISLE OF WIGHT—
FESTIVAL OF LIFE 1970

(In 1970, when I wrote the first drafts of this, I
didn't know that Hendrix & Morrison would die
soon after. Neither did I know that The Who's
searchlights would be the stuff of rock legend. I
didn't write about John B Sebastian, Tiny Tim,
Leonard Cohen and Joni Mitchell being the stars
or Kris Kristofferson being booed off by 600,000.
In the 'arena', with all the fences pulled down, we
existed for three days on a few Ski yoghurts and
the contents of my pipe. Security, safety and
medical services were bizarre too—a few Hells
Angels and what we could do for each other. Yet,
all I could see at the time were colours.)

Blue, yellow, green and reds

Tents

A festival of lives

Scorned for being there

For forgetting

And for giving

Green, pink, grey and oranges

Flags and badges

Their own society

Of love

Weather, hunger, thirst get lost

In togetherness

Yellow, brown, black, white and pinks
Skins and faces
All can't stop smiling
Freedom
I'm an intruder sharing a toy
That will soon be broken

Peace through laughter and song
Such joy isn't legal
Some like spoiling the fun
No chance
Inside
Stuck for days
Constipated
Outside now and hurting
Watching glowing embers
Die

Such joy isn't legal
Some like spoiling the fun
No chance
Memories live on
Ghosts performing raw and wild
Not circus monkeys stealing the stage
Time of their lives
Full colour in black and white era
Live and always live
Despite exiting stage left

Tony Robinson OBE & Taryn Lee Johnston 2021

I SLEPT WITH JIMI HENDRIX
(2020)

Fifty summers ago I was at the 3rd Isle of Wight Festival in search of free love. Free love was made possible by 'the pill'. For two nearly-eighteen-year-olds attending the all-boys, oldest state school in Britain, Beverley Grammar School, this hippie extravaganza promised to be heaven in a box.

I was amazed that 599,998 people came up with the same idea as Phil and me. We boarded the ferry under the dubious protection of Hell's Angels. I never worked out why Hell's Angels were always at the biggest gigs but never liked to ask them.

East Afton Farm became rather crowded. A third more people were there than at Woodstock and four times more than Glastonbury today. There was one stage, no big screen, and no tiny, personal screens to watch the action on.

We had no swimming trunks as skinny dipping was on our 'to do' list. The truth is that nothing on our 'to do' list got ticked off including the free love. But these were joyous days.

I am dyspraxic so I get lost hourly. Phil was great at recognising sheep, cattle and tractors but was lousy at facial recognition. We lost our tent early on. We tried to go to the alluring deep trench latrines twice, but it took many hours to be reunited. On finding a decent spot in the arena on Saturday we stayed there until Monday afternoon. We were happily constipated.
In those days I smoked Three Nuns, not great for the Nuns, and my pipe was in great demand. It would disappear for hours and always taste better when it returned.

The unidentified contents of my pipe and total exhaustion contributed to my shameful incident. The Who's epic reprise of their greatest hits and 'Tommy' had started at 2 am on Sunday. They shone Super Brute searchlights on us to ensure we were awake. The music was then continuously brilliant until gone midnight when the superstar, we had all come to see, appeared.

I saw a tiny figure in a miniscule orange costume, and he opened with 'God Save The Queen' followed by 'Sgt. Pepper's Lonely-Hearts Club Band'. Then I heard Joan Baez singing 'Let it Be'. It was perfect symmetry on Beatles' hits, but I slept with Jimi Hendrix blazing away on stage at his last gig.

My reservations about workplace hugging are not only influenced by my experiences with suffocating relatives. I am in the lowest ten percentile of the population for spatial awareness and physical co-ordination.

A bit like my mate Tony Robbo, I notice that my awkwardness now goes before me and women in particular don't like me getting too close to them. When I enter a room women just smile weakly and wave at me from behind a table, pillar, plant or bystander.

I'm a great supporter of team building as an important part of business life, although again, when I regularly participate with Robbo in such activities as walking over hot coals (at your friend Ant Cracie's events), free fall parachute jumping, white water rafting and even go-kart racing, I'm usually asked to do it miles away from my colleagues. This is because I have a habit of causing injury to others in many unlikely ways, which rather defeats the 'bonding' aspect of the activity.

I admit that when participating in or watching sport, my team mates, friends and family can get a hug of delight from me after an exciting incident. However, I have my doubts that this shared spontaneity, with others you know well, is the same thing as the day-to-day hugging of work colleagues.

What is now being proposed by the occupational psychologists and to be legislated for by Government could create massive absenteeism in small businesses. As the thought of hugging the usual suspects day after day will lead to severe stress and depression in some.

In fact, in the government's promotional film on the value of 'hugging circles', despite their company's business results supposedly having rocketed, most of the men filmed looked scared stiff to me.

It is a behaviour that will encourage your work colleagues who like the 'touchy feely' stuff for either 'warm fuzzy', sexual or barmy reasons.

There is always a work colleague, someone at best eccentric, at worst about to spontaneously combust, who wants to 'release' or 'share' something with you. I prefer them to keep it to themselves, but if you give them any encouragement—

like a hug—I can guarantee they'll be 'releasing'
and 'sharing' all over you.

Indeed, there will come a time in this relationship
when you will find yourself looking after their
four cats, two snakes and the parrot that likes to
be spoken to in piratical, eighteenth century
English whilst both parties wear eye patches. This
is all so the 'huggee' can go away for a much need-
ed break, yet still persecute you with a regular
helping of bizarre postcards and text messages. It
is unlikely in this fraught, depressed, exfoliated
and depilated state that you'll even get placed at
the synchronised swimming championship.
So, is all this potential angst worth it for the sake
of a hug at work? No thanks. I'm just going to take
my turn at making the coffee, buying biscuits and
helping others get their work done. Admittedly
it's a low key way of gaining team harmony,
happiness and increased productivity, but it does
neatly sidestep the parrot!"

He couldn't even rely on himself to do the ordinary things simply and properly. Panic was never far away. He'd find his kettle in the fridge. One day he walked out the apartment and across a pedestrian crossing before he realised he was wearing his PJ bottoms. To be sure not to lose his apartment keys he always has five sets in stock and each day places three sets in different places—bag, hat and back pocket -so that he'll always be able to get back in should he lose some.

Routine just wasn't possible anymore for Chris. Although he'd always been a loner he now felt desperately alone. So, there were so many things to admire in the way this couple got through the day. Their companionship and peace with life were both unattainable for Chris but he never tired of watching them.

The timing and sequence of their daily activities were perfectly replicated. Chris varied the time he entered the park and guessed correctly where each would be in the sequence. The woman always looked content, serene, impeccably dressed, slim, tanned but never too much flesh exposed, short grey hair, designer glasses, straight backed and focused. She seemed to happily and untiringly ingest novel after novel. Chris had never seen her lose her concentration, her focus on the words.

This focus was a remarkable achievement. Serene Lady was never distracted by jumping, skating, stone throwing, biking, tumbling, sobbing, wailing and screaming kids. She never looked up to watch the cooing, coaxing, cajoling and admonishing grandparents. She never shut her book in exasperation from the noise of the pram-wheeling, buggy-pushing, swing pushing, chattering and shouting parents. She never seemed to lose her train of thought as around her feet assembled lizards, fallen kids, over excited dogs and the park's elite guard, of at least one hundred, cats in a variety of superior poses.

Twice in the day this couple would visit the café. They made one or two drinks last for hours. He would do the crossword or suck his pen and listen to his iPod. Serene Lady would recommence reading her novel.

From early to late afternoon they'd move a good fifty metres further up the park. If the cats allowed them, they'd settle at their favourite, adjacent benches. He did not look serene, like his wife, but looked very friendly yet lumpy. Lumpy Lad dressed more like a tourist with the almost obligatory baseball hat to complete the look and for protection too. As his wife resumed her reading position on one bench he would lie down, often flat on his back, sometimes on his side, knees bent, on the other. Within seconds Lumpy Lad was asleep and would stay asleep for forty minutes.

How Chris envied the fact that this man never snored and looked so content in his afternoon nap. Chris could never nap and every night he snored, sweated, hallucinated and woke himself up with the shouting inside his head. Lately he'd seen his mother standing at the end of his bed. She was wearing the nightie she'd worn on the night she died in hospital. Her oxygen mask was dangling from one ear. He heard her complaint, it was always the same, and he always responded to it angrily. By the time his alarm went off at seven each morning he was totally exhausted.

Meanwhile, Serene Lady, on the adjacent bench to the silently sleeping Lumpy Lad, would continue reading her novel. Late in the afternoon the couple would return to the café. He would resume his crossword and she, her novel. They only spoke when they moved locations. At 5.30 each day they left the park, together of course, stopping off at the grocery shop near their apartment.

...

The raging and the effort involved in writing this
down were draining Chris of his energy. He want-
ed to tell Steph more about his project so that she
would respect him but he knew that, for today, he
had nothing left. He'd over used his inhaler. He
could hardly keep his eyes open and even when he
tried to focus, what he'd written was blurred.
He'd start again in the morning. He hated not
telling everything to Steph but there was no
option. He knew what he was doing was for the
right reasons and all he could do was give her
those reasons and hope that she understood when
she found out what he'd done.

He decided to walk further on through Independ-
ence Park to watch the sun set. With luck his
adopted cat, Mr. Bojangles, would be there too.
He'd called the cat Mr. Bojangles not because this
cat could dance or 'jump so high' but because of
the line in the song about Bojangles' dog of fifteen
years. The line was that the dog 'just upped and
died'. Mr. Bojangles had this same effect on dogs.

This was a large white cat with brown markings;
one was on his tail and another as a patch, over
one eye. When an unsuspecting, excitable dog
spied Mr. Bojangles in his favourite sleeping spot,
in the hedgerow, naturally it would bark and
prepare for the chase. Mr. Bojangles did not like
his sleep being disturbed.

It was a great shock to the dog, of any size, to see this large white cat advancing in slow, measured strides towards it. Mr. Bojangles also had a whole range of hard cat gimmicks as he approached the ring. Two of these gimmicks turned every dog's blood to ice. Mr. Bojangles would paw the air with each claw in turn whilst making the most fearful loud hissing sound. The dog immediately understood that Mr. Bojangles was not amused and, worse, was a seeker of a dog damaging, vengeance.

The dog would stop barking and for a second would freeze, with tongue flopped out uselessly and eyes staring incredulously.

Then, sensibly, the dog would turn to leave. The dog's pace would then quicken considerably as he realised that he was being followed, at Usain Bolt-like speed, by Mr. Bojangles. Less than ten seconds later the humans and cats in the park would hear the familiar, anguished sounds of mauled dog. The dog probably survives. Mr. Bojangles is unscathed. He struts back, in measured strides, to resume his place and sleep in the shade of the hedgerow.

Sat on their bench overlooking St Julian's Bay, Mr. Bojangles and Chris watch a ten-metre-wide, strip of sunlight. It is at least a mile long. It starts from the highest point on the horizon—the top of

the blue Portamoso tower. It travels down
through the dusk and then rides on the waves of
the dark sea to rest directly below them. They are
the chosen ones.

On lies couched as truth...

I believe that Tony's 5 years at Amway UK and the guilt he felt when he found out about the unsavoury side of the MLM sector have profoundly influenced his work since. Particularly, his work to get better support for new business owners and his investigations into what he calls 'the business opportunity industry'.

He is keen to point out the ladders to success as a start-up and #happipreneur, for example, 'bootstrap don't borrow', 'test trading and 'multiple income streams' but he is also motivated to expose the snakes that lead to debt and depression.

He has been forthright in his opinions in blogs, interviews and articles. He gets trolled for his views. Even his fictional work references the business opportunity industry. In his most recent novel 'Loose Cannon' there is an MLM senior executive that is being blackmailed by network leaders.

His fictitious satire, with real business tips, 'Freedom from Bosses Forever' exposes how easy it is to get sucked into the scams, fakery, 'get rich quick' and secretive peer pressure groups.

See this conversation between the narrator of 'Freedom from Bosses Forever', Leonora Soculitherz, and a representative of the Tochen Network. They are meeting at the request of Soculitherz' all action, American lover and 'walking on toenails' guru—Ant Cracie.

"But I've never heard of Tochen."

"Cool. Sorry about that. Didn't Ant tell you anything? What do you want to know?"

"Who'll be in the audience?"

"Sure. Well look, there are four branches of the Tochen Network and the majority of the meetings are on a branch by branch basis. The Madrid meeting is for the 'Entrepreneurs' Club' branch. So, members and their guests will all be successful business owners or leaders of industry and commerce—nice people—your kind of people".

"It's not a network or multi-level marketing/ pyramid selling, is it? I hate all that happy-clappy, achieve your dreams, get rich quick rubbish. Anyway, it's illegal in Canada and I am a Canadian citizen."

"No, it's not that at all. I can't deny it's a network, but no one gets commissions for selling anything. Neither can you apply to join it—you have to be invited. Members pay their annual subscriptions to a charity of their choice if they feel they're getting value. Anyone can leave the network at any time.

"Not a religious sect is it?"

"No, although one of the four key values includes 'being Christian'. That only means the network goes by the values prescribed in the Bible. It's quicker than writing some out. In fact, nothing is written—no rules, regulations, agreements or paperwork. It's all about personal development. We just enjoy our networking and enjoy developing. No prayer meetings and no-one has to go to church—I promise!"

"How long have you been in it?"

"No-one says whether they're in it or not. I've just been asked to see if you'd like to speak with Ant at the Madrid event. Look, I have to dash Leonora. Why not have a chat with Ant, see if you want to do it and he'll get hold of me to let me know?"

A good-looking guy, but a bit intense I thought.

Tony and many others believe that the language used to control minds and hearts is the most insidious aspect of both the business opportunity industry and politics today. Lies are dressed up as truths and very quickly become the truth.

...

Q. I know you don't miss the business opportunity and positive thinking scene—why are you so anti the dream builders?
A: Most of us think we're too smart to fall for a way of starting a business which promises success yet doesn't deliver it. That's a mistake as the way business opportunities are sold is ever more sophisticated and the sellers are often the most respectable, even revered, people.

Many famous people claim these ready-made business opportunities provide a safer, proven, route to entrepreneurial success. If you don't succeed, then it'll be because you didn't dream big or you associated with losers or you've got a negative attitude. Anything but the business opportunity is overhyped rubbish.

Because it's overhyped rubbish is why very few make any money out of them. It's why so few succeed through buying self-help books and attending Tony Robbins' seminars.

The people selling the business opportunity, self-help books, DVDs and seminars are totally convincing because they don't see anything wrong in what they're offering and they believe it's your fault if what they're selling doesn't work for you.

These business opportunity sellers are usually salaried employees or just earning money out of being speakers, so my starting question to them is usually "If it's such a good business opportunity why aren't you doing it?"

Q. I saw you do a show where you said avoiding snakes is really important—explain?
A: There are more snakes out there than ladders for people wishing to start a business. If you want to be a #Happipreneur then avoiding the snakes is as important a skill as being very good at what you do, winning customers, managing cash flow and making deals.

The 'follow my way to success, wealth and happiness' business opportunity, positive thinking and self-help industry preys on the most vulnerable in our society.

Everyone needing to make money as quickly as possible, in order to make ends meet is vulnerable. Everyone who believes successful people have 'secrets' to their success, which can be copied, is vulnerable. Everyone who wants a much better lifestyle with all the status trappings—better house, a better car, better holidays—and who doesn't?—is vulnerable.

If you're interested in finding out how the 'dream big' sellers and all the speakers and writers promoting positive thinking and the law of attraction, all of which looks great, can actually cause real harm then google 'American Dream Turned Nightmare' or read 'Smile or Die—How positive thinking fooled America and the World' by the famous American journalist, Barbara Ehrenreich or 'The Antidote' (to positive thinking) by the acclaimed British journalist, Oliver Burkeman or 'Happy' by Derren Brown.

Donald Trump would call Ehrenreich, Burkeman and Brown 'losers' and they haven't written the type of self-help books Oprah Winfrey endorses and promotes on her show—so I promote Ehrenreich, Burkeman and Brown instead!

There are much better ways of earning a living out of your own business, but they all look so much more like hard work. Every successful entrepreneur I know has worked very hard for their success. It's easier to work really hard and build your own business if you're doing something you love and something you're good at.

ON BUSINESS ADVICE

Q: What's the best piece of business advice you've been given?
A: Never have to cross the street to avoid someone.

The best advice I received as a new start-up was from a micro-business owner who ran a successful recruitment and temp agency in Milton Keynes. This was in the mid-eighties—that's the 1980s for those who question which century I was born in. The business owner, Brian, said: "I live, work and play in this community and I'll never do anything which would mean I have to cross the street to avoid someone".

Brian lived and worked in Milton Keynes and being respected by the whole community was the most powerful marketing tool for his business. It also made for a very happy life at work and at play. Positive word of mouth was more influential and lower cost than advertising, direct marketing, PR and employing salespeople.

Q: Over the years you've interviewed a lot of business people, what's one of your pet peeves?
A: When I'm interviewing entrepreneurs I often ask "Give me a tip that you think will be useful for a start-up?". I'm always disappointed if they just repeat one of the motivational quotes we see every day on social media.

At least they should give these guru quotes their own twist. When I'm asked for my tip I often say, "Surround yourself with people who make you giggle". When my parents were running their business, they seemed to be always surrounded by close friends and were always in fits of giggles. The laughter Clare and I have shared in our business is the greatest treasure.

We know that the happiest, longest living people are in countries where they live very simple lives, haven't got wealth and haven't even heard of goal setting. As Bob Dylan said,

"A man is a success if he gets up in the morning and gets to bed at night, and in between he does what he wants to do."

Q: You get a lot of stick on social media, how do you feel about it

A: The trolls go with the territory and I understand why so many businessmen, for it is predominantly men, can't understand why I try to level the playing field to give the smallest of businesses, including all the self-employed, the best possible chance of making ends meet. 'You can't be a socialist and an entrepreneur', they say. I'm not an entrepreneur, but I am a very proud independent business owner and I am a socialist.

The critics' argument goes that I'm supporting 'losers' and unambitious people lacking a positive or 'scale up' mindset. To these businessmen winning is everything and by winning, they mean getting rich. If you're not wealthy it is your own fault.

I understand why my wanting every new business owner to have the very best opportunity of surviving their first three years doesn't chime with 'dream bigger', 'survival of the fittest' and 'fail fast, fail better' mantras.

Q: Why are you not in favour of government funding scale-up support to existing business owners?

A: They always get it wrong. I haven't the time or energy to explain all the mistakes they make, but I must have seen at least 20 government-funded business growth schemes that haven't delivered. Most Government schemes are patronising, to say the least. Most of them believe that big companies, universities and banks can show existing micro-business owners what they're doing wrong and how they can grow their own business. There are an amazing number of people that, without ever having started and run their own business, feel that they can advise micro-business owners how to scale up.

Private sector support is always better quality than these government schemes. My feeling is that the government should only get involved in helping new business owners and much evidence presented to them supports this. Microbusiness owners that have been running their own business for a couple of years are totally capable of deciding what help they need to grow. They can pay for it. Free start-up support should be available as a right.

The Government should get involved in doing things within their control rather than playing God with our livelihoods. So, they can help all micro-business owners reduce costs. It is way too expensive to run a business in the UK in comparison with most other countries. The Government can reduce costs that are killing micro-business owners in such areas as utilities, rates, the cost of regulatory compliance, fast broadband and #PayIn30Days.

ON OBE'S AND LIFE AFTER ESTABLISHMENT

Q: Why did you get an OBE?
A: I can only guess that a senior civil servant or Minister felt that I'd gone the extra mile in working with the government to improve the quality and accessibility of enterprise support and training in the UK. I must admit that by 2001 we thought we had made a lot of progress.

I was voluntarily and unpaid on every one of the most influential policies proposing organisations and forums in the UK. SFEDI standards were underpinning both policy and practice.

When you consider that in 1996 I'd been ashamed of how hopeless the 'owner-manager' standards that we inherited were, then to have revised them and made them useful to underpin all help to start-ups and indie business owners in the UK was a bit of an achievement.

It's still 'Other Buggers' Efforts' though. Clare (business partner), Julie, Stephan and especially, the late John Copsey and his team of assessors, plus the senior civil servants like the late and great Linda Ammon CBE, Derek Carr and Verni Tannam were the heroes. I just did the standing up and sitting down work—all the showing off.

Q: You were in the Establishment then weren't you?

A: I hope not. I was used to being at posh places like the Grosvenor House Hotel and House of Commons from my time at Amway. Clare had ironed out my table manners. But I always thought of myself as being the token micro-business owner that had the research to back their opinions. Most of the people I met at that time were male, private school educated, wealthy and, for some reason, thought that I wasn't a 'life-styler' but a serious thinker. How wrong they were!

Q: Yet you're critical of many entrepreneurs and small business membership organisations that lick the boots of the Government?

A: I understand how it happens and, hey, I'm a Happipreneur so it doesn't bother me much that so many people get sucked into the bubble. The Establishment bubble has fine food, fine wines and the most wonderful places and entertainment to enjoy. It's no different to Amway leading distributors going to luxury hotels in Cannes and Montreux—once you've tasted the prestige and luxury you want more.

For example, Chief Executives of small business membership organisations will enjoy being in the bubble but also can't afford to not be liked by Government and Banks—same thing. Their membership won't be very happy if their CEO is not involved in all the important talks. So, they have to 'welcome' whatever policy announcement comes out even though they know that they're not what they lobbied for.

Similarly, leading entrepreneurs will be asked to Chair Committees for the Government and these entrepreneurs will love how well they're looked after—locations, VIPs, secretariat and comfort. Although these leading entrepreneurs can afford their own luxury they are now mixing with the really powerful.

Remember all our current cabinet of ministers are multi-millionaires but more powerful than any entrepreneur. It's like a drug they don't want to come off. That's why they lend their name to reports and policy recommendations they haven't written. They go native.

I'm no angel. I hate posh clubs, but I still go to Lords to watch cricket, when invited by my friend, a Lords member, and take my champagne through the Grace Gates and meet the dress code of the Warner stand. But I can only do it occasionally. I love being outside the bubble.

Q: But you miss think tanks at Windsor Castle?
A: I was only there for a small number of days on a handful of visits, but they're etched in the memory. A lot of policy forums are under

Chatham House Rules. You're very well looked after in terms of environment and food but of course, you don't get paid. Rituals are very important to the Establishment and I would never breach confidentiality—it's the most important aspect of being trusted. But I really was at my best then.

It was an opportunity for me to contribute at the highest level to small firms policy from the research I've been involved in. There's joy in finding creative solutions to problems. Just a lot of bright people in a room trying to be useful and some of it eventually finds its way into Government policy to benefit the lives of business owners.

It was also a nightmare staying in the Queen and Prince Philip's home. Prince Philip had given St George's House and Library to the pursuit of thought and public endeavour and those lucky enough to be invited there were very well looked after—including an honesty bar. My problem is that it was a home not a hotel so the rooms in St George's House didn't have locks on them and as a dyspraxic, after using the honesty bar, I was tiptoeing up the stairs and gingerly opening many doors before I found my bedroom.

Q: You are known for doing more than is expected of you. Where does this come from?
A: When Clare and I were at our most successful with Business Advisary Bureau we were charging

from £450 right up to £1200 a day for my time. That sounds and is very good but both Clare and I were so desperate to give value for money that we always did many more hours and days than we charged for. One of my obsessions, from being ripped off by solicitors and accountants, was to detail pages and pages of information as to exactly what we'd done for the client in every hour we charged for.

We even detailed the extra hours we weren't charging for. The accounts departments in the large companies that were our clients weren't at all interested in this detail, but there was some good psychology behind what we were doing. The first recipient of the invoice is the executive in the company that we worked with and nearly always these invoices require a second signature of their boss before it goes to accounts. We gave such detailed information that the executive would look great in the organisation as to the value for money that he'd achieved from contracting with the BAB.

Clare made it her business to know who in the company was signing off our invoice and who in the accounts department would be processing it. We rarely had a problem in being paid promptly—certainly #PayIn30Days. Very few people are brave enough to lie to Clare. Eventually, on many contracts we asked for a third up front, a third on delivery and a third within 14 days. As these clients knew we always delivered more than they asked for we became able to dictate our payment terms rather than theirs.

Q: Were you looking to slow down and retire in Scarborough?

A: No, I haven't met many micro-business owners who look to retire. I had the view that 57 would be about my life expectancy, the age my father died, so I certainly wasn't looking to slow up. I wanted to achieve more and faster, but not in a wealth-producing way. I certainly wanted to do a lot more creatively, especially with fictional writing.

It's ironic that I've lost so many friends that were 57 or under and here I am still. I'm so lucky and live every day to the full as happily as I can. While I have my marbles, that's debatable I know, I'll always have to earn money as Carl doesn't work or claim any benefits and Alan earns very little from online trading. Eileen has now retired from the Hull University library after 18 years in a job she loved and was loved by the students.

So, it's up to me. There may even be a last downsizing around the corner if we move to Ireland where Eileen would like to live. I'm so lucky if it ends tomorrow, I've had a wonderful time and I learned how to enjoy every day.

ON INSPIRATION AND EARLY ENTREPRENEURS

Q—Who would you suggest was one of the earliest entrepreneurs?

A: You'll love this.

There are many different types of writer; freelance journalists, scriptwriters, fiction—many genres, non-fiction, including travel, sport, business, magazines, blogs, speeches, podcasts, magazines, social media content—playwrights and songwriters.

Charles Dickens was many of these types of writers and, if the technology had been available, would have been an actor, film director, TV star, TED Talker, a major social media influencer, documentary writer, global investigative journalist, blogger and podcaster. As well as being one of the greatest writers of all time he was one of the greatest entrepreneurs ever in the creative arts.

Bob Dylan, a Nobel Prize winner for literature, is a modern day equivalent and Dylan is, despite his lyrics, a happy entrepreneur. For most of his adult life Charles Dickens pursued his passions but always so that he could make money. He made a difference to the world through his social commentary, campaigns, charitable enterprises, editorship and investigative journalism but never lost his adoring public from every walk of life. Politicians read Dickens and knew they had to act on what he wrote.

What made Dickens so successful, like Dylan, was that

he was a great entertainer—maybe the greatest. Dylan's never-ending tour of gigs is as exhausting but as essential to his continued success as Dickens' 100-night reading tours in theatres. Most successful entrepreneurs, in all sectors, realise they must be engaged with their audience, almost in the same way as an entertainer. They will develop multiple income streams from the audience they are engaged with.

For example, compare two of my all-time five favourite writers, because I loved the satire in their later work, Charles Dickens and Herman Melville. Herman's first two novels were very successful, so much so that he was able to buy a very nice property for his family and work as a full-time, self-employed, writer. He peaked too early. He had no more successful novels, col-lec-tions of short stories and poetry in his lifetime.

My favourite, now regarded as classic, Melville novels and novellas such as Moby Dick, The Confidence Man, Bartleby the Scrivener, Benito Cereno and Billy Budd (published posthumously) made him so little money that he had to get a job. He worked as a full-time civil servant, in Cus-toms, for over twenty years before retiring.

Melville kept promising his publishers more romantic travel tales like his first two novels, but he never delivered. Unlike Dickens, who always delivered, it is likely that Melville either didn't really know his audience or, more likely, didn't want to write what his audience would buy.

Compare Melville with Dickens. Compare Melville with Brad Burton—writer of motivational business books, or Gary Vaynerchuk the Brad Burton equiva-lent in the US and Globally.

Whatever the changes to the world of publishing (books or music) or changes to the algorithms on Facebook, Twitter or LinkedIn it is a fact that Dickens, Dylan, Burton and Vaynerchuk remain fully engaged with their audience who continue to buy their books and flock to see them perform.

In fact, no creative entrepreneur has ever done 'engagement' better than Dickens. How did he do it? Why does it work just as well today?

Aged 29, a Londoner, Charles Dickens was given the freedom of the city of Edinburgh. This took place in the summer of 1841. He went to the theatre, after one of the many large—(hundreds ate, and hundreds watched them eat from the balconies)—and lavish dinners in his honour. The audience, warned by the newspapers that 'Boz' would be present, crammed in to see him. As he entered the orchestra struck up 'Charley is my darling'.

His extraordinary popularity in the UK and USA increased year by year through to his death at 58. No organisation, company, publisher, agent, manager or publicist could have achieved this level of audience engagement for Charles Dickens. Charles Dickens, the entrepreneur-writer achieved it by his own actions to build his own brand around his unique personality and talents.

The brand loyalty for an individual usually lasts longer and is stronger than a company, product or service. Charlie Mullins OBE is Pimlico Plumbers. Kanya King CBE is the MOBO Awards and Antony Chesworth is EKM. Stormzy is Stormzy. Boz was Charles Dickens.

Like most entrepreneurs I've met who have made their name out of doing something remarkably well—Chris Percival as a para medic, Antony Chesworth building online shops, Charlie Mullins out of plumbing—formal education played a very minor part in their learning. Dickens was almost totally self-taught in everything he excelled at. He read voraciously and loved learning how to perform.

The imaginative world, such as 'The Arabian Nights' and 'Don Quixote' was important to him. As stated earlier, my favourite satirical novel, by Dickens is 'Hard Times' and in it he suggests individual 'fancy' (imagination and creativity) is the way to personal fulfilment and happiness whereas, process, facts (data), automation, factories and commerce are the way to greed, bullying, corruption and misery. Individual enterprise is most often good and institutional production is most often bad.

I don't know whether Schumacher read Dickens, but I know he would have approved.

Schumacher made it clear that politicians and shareholders pre-occupation with increasing GDP and productivity were only likely to create stressed out, unhappy workers.

Dicken's genius was to teach himself how to write from the imagination and create characters which have never been surpassed in literature. Some of these characters are like you and me. By putting them in situations we have not experienced—a debtor's prison; a court of law; a gang of thieves; a revolution; a textile factory—we are forced to consider the rights and wrongs of their treatment by the state. Fiction led to social reform and, even, the family Christmas as we now know it.

His success as an entrepreneur, like most entrepre-neurs, was based, not on positive attitude or mindset, but on street-smart understanding of what he could make and sell within the realities of affordable costs and positive cashflow. Positive cash flow was a motivating force for the workaholic Dickens as he was haunted by the Debtors' prison which his father was sent to. His mother and siblings joined his father in the prison, but he was banished, as a 12-year-old, to work in a blacking factory and pay his way.

Today's equivalent to the debtor's prison is credit scoring. It is easier to escape the constraints of prison than it is to escape a low credit score in this digital-by-default world.

Dickens was renowned for immense physical energy and perseverance. Dickens taught himself how to write and do shorthand which led to apprentice journalist jobs, latterly as a parliamentary reporter. But he wanted to be successful in the imaginary world. He nearly became an actor and wrote many short stories which he submitted and had rejected before, after years of trying, at 22, a short comic fictional sketch was accepted by a magazine.

Six more sketches followed, and the magazine took him on in a job. Dickens continued to write street sketches of London and started to build his own brand whilst in a job by using the pseudonym 'Boz'. The illustrator he used for most of his life took the pseudonym of 'Phiz' to go with 'Boz'.

Dickens was fully independent by the age of 23 and built his brand further by his flamboyant dress. He was renowned for his blue cloak with velvet facings and brightly coloured, fancy waistcoats.

He learned, rather like test trading and crowd funding combined, that he could publish a novel in monthly numbers of a magazine and build the audience by getting feedback from the readers as the tension mounted and the public asked for more about certain characters.

Dickens, like most entrepreneurs, took on more work than he could handle once having promised three novels to three different publishers while writing a stage play and a libretto for an opera. Like most entrepreneurs he eventually found a way to control his own destiny and not be controlled as much by his customers (publishers).

He founded, created and edited his own weekly and monthly magazines. As soon as he could he took the Boz mania' on tour to the USA and Canada.

Eventually he was making more money from touring with his 'readings' (£33,000 in 1866 – 1868 when £300 a year was a good salary) than his prolific, financially successful and critically acclaimed novel writing. All achieved through mass entertainment with no need for mindset mayhem or hot coals walking—Tony Robbins eat your heart out.

THE SOCULITHERZ'
INCREDIBLE
CHOCO-WINE DIET
AN EXPLANATION
BY TONY ROBINSON OBE

HISTORY AND SCIENCE

Soculitherz (pronounced 'so-cool-it-hurts') is best known in the UK for co-writing, with Tony Robinson OBE, the satire 'Freedom from Bosses Forever'. However, in her native Canada she is known as a celebrity, fashionista, investigative journalist, owner of a single celebrity name, like Beyoncé and Batman, and as the creator of the 'Incredible Choco-Wine Diet'.

Whilst Jamie Oliver was improving the nutritional value of school dinners in Britain, Leonora Soculitherz was raising the bar of her nation's well-being by perfecting chocolate and wine combining.

The health and rejuvenation benefits of chocolate (since Amazonian times—5000 BC) and red wine (since men and women found grape) are well known. New scientific studies emerge every year which explain why they work.

Yet, it was only when Soculitherz discovered an ancient Greek recipe book by Plato's younger sister, Plate, that the power of coupling became clear. Most Greeks wouldn't have known this coupling power either as discovering new truths was the province of old men in white dresses with dodgy beards. No-one would listen to a woman named after a river or a piece of crockery.

CHOCO-WINE CALORIE COUNTING AND COMBINING

Ditch the iPad and carry a tablet of dark chocolate bars around with you. Make your tablet by getting six equal sized chocolate bars. Put tape around the six bars and then use as a measuring stick. Measure your chocolate consumption against it (cake and syrup are tricky).

Soculitherz recommends you drink a third of a glass of red wine with half a bar's worth of chocolate and half a bottle of red wine with three bars worth.

Do not eat the bars, except in an emergency, from your tablet/measuring stick or else you'll get confused about the precise, scientific quantities of chocolate intake to match with your wine intake.

Discount, that is FORGET, about Choco Wine calories if you are calorie counting. Why? The net effect from balancing your chocolate and red wine consumption each day is NOTHING—got it?—nothing, nought, zero and zip. As Plate said in her ancient recipe book, "You cannot live by wine alone. Add some chocolate".

Develop your taste for dark chocolate and red wine in the *acclimatisation phase*. This essential phase is comprised of a weekend in bed with box sets, a case of Rioja and a large sack of dark chocolate products.

DISCIPLINE

Some moaning Minnies and Mikes complain that they just don't feel like chocolate and wine for breakfast. Soculitherz and I don't start the day with breakfast, for very different reasons—Soculitherz would not admit to undue flatulence. But millions have breakfast as a result of propaganda by the bacon and eggs producers and breakfast cereal manufacturers. Breakfast on the choco-wine diet may be tough to take but if you want to look as good as Soculitherz you have to choco-wine balance every meal.

Here are a few breakfast tips that I've gleaned from Choco-Wine Diet devotees: Add water to your wine like the ancient Greeks did (yuk). Coat all manner of breakfast healthy stuff with a thick dark chocolate coating. There are many recipes on the Choco-Wine Diet Pinterest site including raspberry panacotta with dark chocolate and almond cheesecake with dark chocolate. Do remember that grapes and cocoa are both fruits so be careful not to exceed your five a day

EXERCISE

Soculitherz has suffered some harsh criticism of her ICW diet. The main beef (note that wine is fat-free, cholesterol free, gluten-free and dairy free) with her diet is that it does not include exercise.

Soculitherz believes that if you rigorously follow her diet, you'll have so much fun and be so irresistible you'll get plenty of exercise. Sweaty armpits have no place in the life of a Canadian fashionista!

However, for those that just can't quit the exercise addiction here are two optional exercises you can try. Handily, the first exercise can be done in the secrecy of your own home. Make two barbells of, say, six fine Belgian chocolate bars, a bit like how you made the tablet/measuring stick. Raise to your chin five times and take a break eating one of the bars. Repeat until all six bars have been eaten. No pain, no gain.

The second exercise requires a bit more planning but there is a photo on the Pinterest site of me and my friend Bob doing this exercise and you can see it's worth it. We went to a vineyard in the Rioja region of Spain but I'm sure you could do it in your local supermarket. You'll need a lot of grapes in a roomy container and you stamp on them with your bare feet. After the wine stomping you can drink the fruits of your labour.

CHEATING

ChocoWinefulness is very similar to mindfulness. Instead of experiencing the moment stuff through your breathing you do the same experiencing stuff with each bite or sip.

But there are times when all this discipline, balancing and focus on the Incredible Choco Wine diet just sucks. It can test your patience and, frankly, you just want to have a bucket of prosecco or binge on cinder toffee ice cream.

Holidays, including Christmas and Easter, are such times when you really want to cheat. Here are my three favourite cheats which you can do at any time of the year:

1) Only half cheat, for example, by substituting another type of wine. This is fine as a one-off and that includes prosecco and anything alcoholic with wine it—pour some wine in your cider if necessary.

2) Eat a replacement dessert or pud that isn't predominantly chocolate. My fave is cinder toffee ice cream but I make it all OK on the ICW Diet by sticking a chocolate flake with chocolate sprinkles on it and having a chocolate cone.

3) Keep and count your corks. Then if you find it's less than 90 corks over a three-month period you can have some 1.5 or 2 bottle days as a reward. You can justifiably do the same with chocolate bar wrappers with a case of large dark chocolate Toblerone as your reward.

FREQUENTLY ASKED QUESTIONS

Q: If I've drunk too much wine in the day is there a way of not balancing it with more chocolate. I feel sick.
(Mrs Wan, Bognor Regis, Sussex)
A: No. As you well know Soculitherz refuses to speak to me because she thinks I'm an idiot. I've told you before, rules are rules—I can't get them changed.

Q: Why don't all GPs prescribe your wonderful diet? If they did, I could claim it on expenses. (I. Grabbitt MP, House of Commons, London)
A: The good news is that when the transition from the NHS to an American owned healthcare system is complete you will be able to mitigate your expense.

The bad news is that in the interim the ICW Diet will be more expensive. This is because more chocolate products and alcohol will be sourced from American owned companies rather than, say, French, Spanish and Belgian producers.

Fortunately, compulsory healthcare and welfare (including pensions) insurance collected directly by Government from employers and employees, as part of the digital taxation roll out, will mitigate this cost. The ICW Diet may be classified as an essential repeat prescription, like asthma inhalers and insulin. The cost will be covered by premium healthcare insurance schemes. G4S, Capita, Atos, Maximus, Virgin and the rest of the UK's future health, welfare, prison, security and social care providers will be paid directly by the Government's healthcare insurance providers.

As your employer is the government and as you earn a great deal more than the minimum, £60,000 a year, it is likely you will be in a non-contributory, premium healthcare insurance scheme. You will be able to get your ICW Diet

components through your contactless 'member-
ship' payment card.

There is no need for you to make an expenses
claim. Good news for you but Soculitherz is not
happy. Soculitherz believes the US manufacturers
will rip off the British public which will make her
ICW Diet less accessible and more elitist. In
Canada, essential drugs such as insulin and
asthma inhalers are one fifth of the price of those
in the USA, which is why poorer Americans, not
covered by an employer's healthcare insurance,
cross the border to buy insulin.

**Q: I know that exercise is optional but I'm a
keen tennis player. Will your diet help me and
my doubles partner to win more games?
(Lord Murray, House of Lords, London).**
A: I've no idea, your Lordship.

**Q. 70% cocoa chocolate is an acquired
taste which I haven't acquired. What are
the alternatives?
(Ms Takun, Lewes, Sussex)**
A: I regularly post alternatives on the Soculitherz
Incredible Choc-Wine Diet @Pinterest board

**Q: Soculitherz is my all-time favourite A-list
celebrity. Has she any plans to make a movie
about her life and the Choco-wine diet?
(your daughter, Sinead)**
A: No.

**Q: Is there a support group?
(your wife, Eileen)**
A: No

THE SOCULITHERZ AND ROBINSON COLLABORATION

The collaboration between Leonora Soculitherz (pronounced So-Cool-It Hurts) and Tony (pronounced Turney) Robinson started in 2004 with the production of a book entitled 'Buzzing with the Entrepreneurs—18 years and up for it'. The book was produced as a gift for the 200 guests attending the 18th anniversary celebration of the Business Advisory Bureau Limited (BAB) at the Café Royal in London.

The Business Advisory Bureau Limited was co-founded and co-owned by Robinson and Clare Francis and founded many other enterprises in its, eventual, 32-year history including the Sales Qualifications Board, SFEDI and Entrepreneurs UK. Robinson is known in the UK as the Micro Business Champion for his campaigns, including #PayIn30Days, talks and shows. He co-founded with Tina Boden, the #MicroBizMatters movement and the annual #MicroBizMatters Day. He founded and curates The Small is Beautiful Roll of Honour.

Socuiltherz was in the UK promoting her autobi-
ography 'Over Strung and Under Nourished'
when she was asked by the BAB to write 'Buzzing'.
Clare Francis was a fan of her weekly columns on
fashion, self-fulfilment and nutrition. She also felt
that Robinson and Soculitherz may have a lot in
common; both were English Literature graduates,
fans of the Bronte sisters, known for their
unusual dress and had similar upbringings—
Soculitherz in Hull, Ottawa, Canada and Robin-
son in Hessle, Hull, Yorkshire. Francis underesti-
mated the communication difficulties—Robinson
is incomprehensible.

Soculitherz described her first experience of
working with Robinson as "unforgettable" and of
Robinson as 'a world class, badly dressed idiot
who can't go two minutes without spilling a drink
over me'. In 2009 enticed by a large advance, she
came back to the UK, for forty days, to investigate
the government and entrepreneurship. This
resulted in the book 'Stripping for Freedom'. Four
years later, 'Stripping for Freedom' was improved
and updated by Robinson. It became the best-sell-
ing satire, **'Freedom from Bosses Forever'**, much
to the disgust of Soculitherz.

'Soculitherz on TV—20 Feisty Enterprise Tips'
was published in 2016, without the consent of the
reclusive Soculitherz (by now a single celebrity
name like Beyoncé, Cher, Rihanna and Elvis). In

'Soculitherz on TV' Robinson used the transcripts of six interviews with Soculitherz, in a never-aired TV series, to produce a short guide for start-ups. Robinson realised the potential of the Soculitherz' Incredible Choco-Wine Diet after trying it himself.

In truth, Robinson and Soculitherz stopped collaborating in 2009 when as her self-appointed agent he arranged a UK tour for her in 'inappropriate venues'. Soculitherz refused to tour or wear the costumes and they have not spoken, except through lawyers, since.

THE
HAPPIPRENEUR
A Memoir
& Guide For
Enterprising
People
BY TONY ROBINSON OBE
& TARYN LEE JOHNSTON
Foreword by Tim Campbell MBE

THE HAPPIPRENEUR—
TONY ROBINSON OBE &
TARYN LEE JOHNSTON

'The massive debts, poverty, business closures, mental health issues, even suicides are heart-breaking since lockdown. But running your own enterprise is still a happier and more fulfilling option than many of the rubbish jobs now on offer."

Walking with the entrepreneurs

Both authors agree that no-one can afford to wait for the revolution any more than they can afford to wait for a vaccine. Johnston explained: 'As business owners, Tony, myself and all our readers have to just get on with it. It is always a roller-coaster and we expect the unexpected. We hope our guide helps them to avoid the snakes and climb the ladders.

Tony's story of what he has learned from his own businesses and working with many famous entre-preneurs is important for others to know. It is about how to live an enterprising and happy life. We answer the questions 'How to become a Happipreneur?' and 'Why #MicroBizMatters?'. We call out the fakes and the scammers and provide a blueprint for the Establishment on why and how they can level the playing field."

Taryn's story is in many ways an example of how you CAN grow and achieve happiness in your own business. Starting her own business ten years ago, as a single mother of two boys, Taryn decided that it was the best way to ensure she had time for her children as well as being able to provide for them. She has been through all of the ups and downs discussed in this book and at the time of writing owns three successful companies as well as being a university lecturer.

There is no other book like this, incorporating both the biography of a champion of micro-business and a guide for all those making their own way out of corporate life.

Out now from all good bookstores

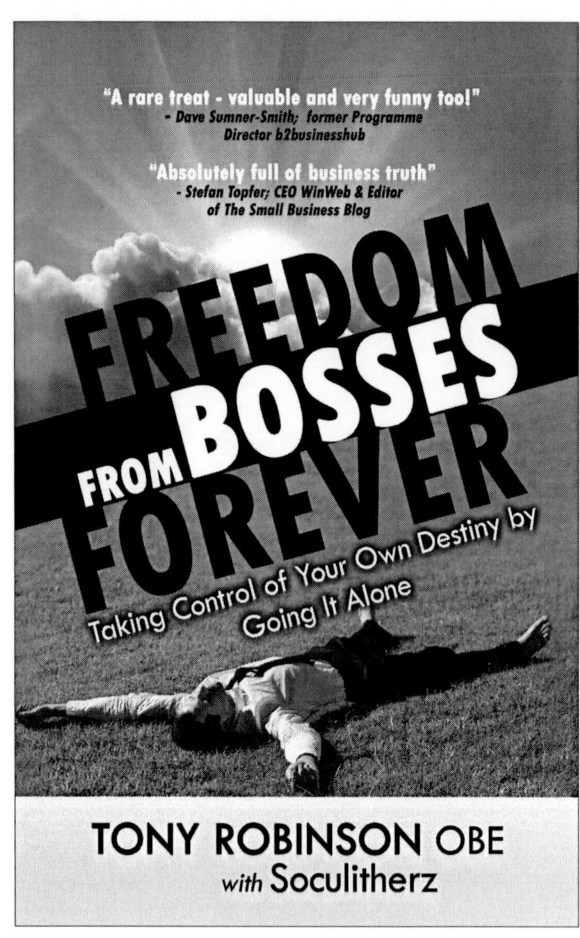

"A rare treat - valuable and very funny too!"
- Dave Sumner-Smith; former Programme Director b2businesshub
"Absolutely full of business truth"
- Stefan Topfer; CEO WinWeb & Editor of The Small Business Blog
FREEDOM FROM BOSSES FOREVER
Taking Control of Your Own Destiny by Going It Alone
TONY ROBINSON OBE
with Soculitherz

FREEDOM FROM BOSSES FOREVER—
TONY ROBINSON OBE

Freedom from Bosses Forever is a book every lover of satire will enjoy, even if they are not interested in starting and running their own business. It has been described as unique by many reviewers and critics because the characters that appear in it are fictional apart from the much derided Tony Robinson OBE.

'Snorting with laughter' is not an unusual listener reaction.

The fictional fashionista, and narrator of the story, Leonora Soculitherz (So-cool-it-hurts) takes the listener on a journey of discovery. Soculitherz investigates a government and big business conspiracy whilst unearthing, along the way, the bare essentials of 'own business' success.

Available on Audible Now

TOP TEN TIPS FOR STARTING YOUR OWN BUSINESS— *TONY ROBINSON OBE & NIGEL HUDSON*

Tony's "Ten Terrific Tips" is for anyone looking to start-up and earn a living by working for themselves, such as a sole trader, self-employed person or a micro business owner.

It's based on experience—three decades of starting and running our own businesses and helping other people do likewise.

Simple and short—based on 10 essential tips

Practical help—to apply the tips to your business and extra real-life guidance

Coming 2022